INTRODUCTION

The United States Department of Defense (DoD) budget for Fiscal Year (FY) 2014 requests $526.6 billion to protect and advance security interests at home and abroad during the coming fiscal year and into the future. This budget reflects the difficult choices involved with protecting America's security interests and role as a global power at a time of declining budgets and ongoing fiscal uncertainty about the future. This request balances the competing and compelling demands of supporting troops still engaged in Afghanistan, protecting readiness, modernizing the military's aging weapons inventory, and sustaining the quality and care of the all-volunteer force — all while implementing and deepening our alignment to the Defense Strategic Guidance signed by the President last year. This paper highlights the Department's ongoing efforts to achieve an agile and ready force while maintaining the right capabilities and capacity to rapidly deal with contingencies across the globe.

The Drawdown Continues

The DoD is experiencing declining budgets that have already led to significant ongoing and planned reductions in military modernization, force structure, personnel costs, and overhead expenditures.

The Department estimates a 20 percent drop in the overall defense budget — including declining war costs — from the post-9/11 peak in 2010 to 2017. The Budget Control Act (BCA) of 2011 required total projected defense spending to decline by $487 billion from FY 2012 through 2021. When measured in real terms against the growing cost of personnel, health care, and weapons, this represents a marked decrease in defense purchasing power compared to the past decade.

Sequestration, if allowed to continue, would represent about an 18 percent decline in the inflation-adjusted defense base budget between 2010 and 2014. Sequestration would further reduce average annual defense spending by more than $50 billion each year through FY 2021. To achieve such rapid savings, the Department would first have to target accounts that yield the most immediate savings — modernization programs, training, and maintenance accounts. Additional savings from overhead efficiencies, reducing personnel costs, and structural reforms are possible, but would take much longer to realize.

Modernization Challenges

The military entered the current drawdown in a substantially different position than was the case at the end of the Cold War. Because the 1980s defense build-up was primarily a procurement build-up — the force did not grow in size nor was it deployed substantially more — the military began the 1990s drawdown with a mostly re-capitalized inventory of weapons and equipment. These Reagan-era platforms, however effective, are reaching the end of their service lives and must be replaced in some form, especially the air-superiority and sea-power capabilities called for by the 2012 strategic guidance. Replacing these aging systems with new platforms will require considerable resources.

Whereas during the 1990s drawdown America's primary geo-political adversary had just collapsed, today America faces an increasing array of potential challenges to its national security. Despite the substantial savings made possible by the end of major troop deployments in Iraq and Afghanistan, the ongoing challenges to stability posed by North Korea, Iran, international terrorism and other potential adversaries — though not existential threats on a par with the former Soviet Union — suggest that a "peace dividend" created by a more tranquil global environment is unlikely. Even before sequestration the military services struggled to meet regional commanders' requests for forces, especially carriers, destroyers, and amphibious capabilities for deployment near the Middle East and Asia-Pacific. Consequently, any substantial defense savings in the future must come from the Department's ability to manage risk, readiness, and requirements in a fundamentally different way than the U.S. military has been accustomed to since the end of the Cold War.

The President's defense budget submission for FY 2014 (PB14) reflects decisions made across the following areas, each of which will be discussed further in this paper:
- Act as Good Stewards of Taxpayer Dollars
- Implement & Deepen Program Alignment to New Strategic Guidance
- Seek a Ready Force
- People are Central

For more detailed information on specific capability areas and choices made in the Department's FY 2014 budget submission, annexes are provided at the end of this document.

ACT AS GOOD STEWARDS OF TAXPAYER DOLLARS

<u>Making Every Defense Dollar Count</u>

Recognizing that the inevitable downturn of post-9/11 defense spending would require even more rigorous budget choices, the department leadership between 2009 and 2011 recommended (and the Congress enacted) curtailing or cancelling more than 30 modernization programs — including the Air Force's F-22 fighter aircraft, the Army's Future Combat System, the Navy's next generation destroyer, and the Marine Corps' new amphibious vehicle. These and a number of other major programs had, to varying degrees, experienced unsustainable cost growth, faced serious technological challenges, and even if built to completion, would have provided capabilities in excess of real-world needs that would crowd out other, higher priority investments.

The department also began reducing overhead costs within the military services and across the defense enterprise — by an estimated $200 billion between FY 2012 and FY 2017 — as a result of paring back excess staff, headquarters structures (including a 4-star "combatant command"), general and flag officers, senior civilian executives, and duplication in information technology, intelligence, public affairs, and facilities.

In response to the National Defense Authorization Act (NDAA) for FY 2013 the Department is shrinking its civilian workforce (<u>Annex C</u>), realizing a reduction in civilian personnel of about five percent between FY 2012 and 2018. About half of these reductions depend on infrastructure consolidation, restructuring of military treatment facilities, and forecasted reductions in demand for depot maintenance as we come out of Afghanistan.

<u>Fiscal Year 2014 Request</u>

A guiding principle of DoD budget choices is to first seek efficiencies and target excess overhead costs before cutting military capabilities such as force structure or modernization investments. In the process of developing the FY 2014 budget, the DoD identified about $34 billion in savings over the next five years by more disciplined use of existing resources, including:
- Expanding IT consolidation efforts at the Defense Information Systems Agency (DISA)
- Favoring facility restoration over new construction
- Requesting new infrastructure consolidation

As part of its overall effort to reduce the civilian workforce, the Department has planned reductions in the Military Health System (MHS) totaling 5,235 full time equivalents, or about eight percent, from FY 2012 to FY 2018. Reductions could be over eight thousand full time equivalents depending on future decisions regarding clinical infrastructure, public health, mental health, and wounded warrior care.

Additionally, in FY 2014 the Department reassessed its investments within portfolios and shifted funding to better balance new development and legacy equipment modernization. For example, by choosing a single supplier among industry competitors earlier than planned for the acquisition of the Department's Ground Combat Vehicle (GCV), the Department will preserve the GCV development schedule while reinvesting over $2.5 billion of savings in legacy vehicles to maintain a modern, diverse portfolio of ground vehicle assets.

In other cases, where applicable, the Department used evolutionary approaches to develop new capabilities instead of relying on leap-ahead gains in technology. For example, the Department:

- Moved investment away from the SM-3 IIB interceptor — a high-risk, expensive, late to need system — to improve the capabilities of existing missile defense systems, and investing in research and development for an SM-3/ground-based midcourse interceptor common kill vehicle, resulting in net savings of about $600 million during the Five-Year Defense Program (FYDP).
- Cancelled the precision tracking space sensor — another high-risk project — saving $1.9 billion during the FYDP; the Department invested a portion of these savings in technology upgrades to existing ground-based radars and sensors (Annex I).

In its FY 2013 budget submission, the Department proposed changes to military compensation that would have represented just one-tenth of the BCA-imposed $487 billion of budget reductions, but many of these proposals were rejected by Congress in the FY 2013 NDAA. In FY 2014, the Department resubmitted a new package of military compensation proposals that takes into consideration Congressional concerns from FY 2013. None of the new proposals would result in a reduction in pay or benefits; they simply reduce the rate of growth. The specific proposals include:

- A modest reduction in the growth of military pay by implementing a one percent pay raise for service members in FY 2014.
- A modest additional increase in TRICARE fees and pharmacy co-pays. Where applicable, these fee and co-pay increases would be phased-in and have maximum limits to allow service members and retirees to adjust accordingly. Where appropriate, they are also "grandfathered."

IMPLEMENT & DEEPEN PROGRAM ALIGNMENT TO NEW STRATEGIC GUIDANCE

Spending reductions on the scale required by the Budget Control Act could not be accommodated through improving efficiency and reducing overhead. Cuts to capabilities — force structure and modernization programs — are required as well. The strategic guidance issued in January 2012 set the priorities and parameters that inform those budget choices.

These shifts not only recognize the changing nature of the conflicts in which the U.S. must prevail, but also leverage new concepts of operation enabled by advances in space, cyberspace, special operations, precision-strike, and other capabilities.

Although the force will be smaller, it will employ both lessons from recent conflicts and new technologies developed to confront the most lethal and disruptive threats of the future. Meeting the requirements of the new strategic guidance entailed increasing funding for a few key capabilities while protecting others at existing levels or making comparatively modest reductions. Inevitably, investing in these high-priority areas requires deeper offsetting reductions in areas of lesser priority.

We continue to put a premium on rapidly deployable, self-sustaining forces — such as submarines, long-range bombers, and carrier strike groups — that can project power over great distance and carry out a variety of missions. These choices are consistent with the strategic emphasis on the Asia Pacific and the Middle East, but are applicable anywhere on the globe where U.S. national security interests are threatened.

The strategic guidance and corresponding program choices were reflected in the FY 2013 defense budget request. For FY 2014, this alignment between budget priorities and the major tenets of the strategy was implemented and strengthened.

In FY 2014, the Department continued to *shift to a smaller, leaner force that is agile, flexible, and ready to deploy quickly.* In keeping with the 2012 defense strategic guidance, DoD is no longer sizing U.S. forces for prolonged, large-scale stability operations. The DoD continued its planned drawdown of ground forces, reducing force structure in areas of lower risk to sustain other, higher priority capabilities. The active Army will decline to 490,000 by FY 2017 — slightly higher than its pre-9/11 size — and the active Marine Corps will decline to 182,100 by FY 2017 — a reduction of 76,000 and 20,000, respectively, since FY 2010. Consistent with the new strategy's guidance to provide more responsive maritime forces, the U.S. Navy's active rolls will grow by 3,400 personnel to 326,100 by FY 2018. Naval Reserve end strength will decline 2,500 over the next five years due to the declining demand for specialized assets such as construction units in Afghanistan (Annex D).

In considering the appropriate active/reserve component mix of forces (Annex G), the department evaluated cost, military effectiveness, and availability. Other factors include peacetime and wartime demands, deployment frequency and duration, speed of response, and unit readiness.

In the Reserve Component, the Army National Guard will decrease by 8,000 to 350,000 during FY 2012 — 2016, while authorizations in the U.S. Army Reserve will decrease by 1,000 to a total of 205,000. There will be no change to the Marine Corps reserve.

The DoD is also resubmitting several proposals from its FY 2013 budget submission that were rejected by the Congress, including the retirement of 7 Aegis cruisers and 2 amphibious ships during the FYDP. Despite the military's strategic shift to the Asia-Pacific — a mostly maritime theater — the high costs of maintaining these older ships relative to their capabilities argued strongly for their retirement. While recognizing the budget risk and political difficulties of this course of action, the current fiscal environment leaves the DoD little choice but to continue targeting capabilities that are excess to strategic requirements and warfighting needs.

Working with Congress, the Department re-crafted an Air National Guard (ANG) proposal for its FY 2014 submission that included some of the reductions that were part of the FY 2013 budget submission. In response to state and congressional concerns about the extent of FY 2013 reductions to the ANG, the Department added back 44 aircraft to the ANG, 30 aircraft to the Air Force Reserve, and is taking away 31 aircraft from the active Air Force. To be clear, these shifts were forced by political realities, not strategy or analysis. Our position continues to be that retaining excess air capacity in the reserve component is an unnecessary expenditure of government funds that detracts from more pressing military priorities.

In FY 2014, the Department funded key aspects of the *rebalance to the Asia-Pacific region* by:
- Creating a more operationally resilient Marine Corps presence in the Pacific, undertaking key presence initiatives in Australia, and investing in Guam as a joint strategic hub (Annex H)
- Adding electronic attack EA-18Gs (Growlers) to offset the loss of retired Marine Corps EA-6B (Prowler) squadrons
- Investing in an array of critical munitions, particularly for countering anti-access/area denial (A2/AD) strategies (Annex F)
- Increasing our joint and combined training capacity in and around Guam

- Adding a fourth attack sub to Guam in FY 2015
- Funding airfield resiliency measures such as dispersal, runway repair, and hardening
- Investing in key technologies to defeat anti-access/area denial (A2/AD) capabilities; in particular, the Department continued its investments in the Joint Strike Fighter (JSF), Virginia submarine payload modules, and new bomber programs

The Department *protected and prioritized key investments in technology and new capabilities*:
- *Cyber security* — repurposed and added manpower to create cyber teams dedicated to defend military networks, provide operational support to regional commanders, and to assist civil authorities (Annex B)
- *Space* — rebalanced portfolio to focus on space defense, offense, and its ability to "operate through" a contested environment (Annex A)
- *Airborne Intelligence, Surveillance, and Reconnaissance (AISR)* — invested in both sea-based and extended range, land-based ISR platforms (Annex K)
- *Command, Control, and Communications (C3)* — invested in resilient communications
- *Industrial Base* — funded additional resiliency and responsiveness in critical technology, development, and production areas (Annex M)
- *Energy* — continued to invest in capabilities that reduce the operational risks and growing costs associated with the military's energy consumption (Annex L)

In response to recent threat developments in North Korea and Iran, the Department enhanced *defense of the homeland* against ballistic missiles by increasing the number of fielded Ground Based Interceptors (GBIs) and upgrading the missile field at Fort Greely Alaska.

The FY 2014 request continues to fund key programs that *build partnerships and strengthen key alliances* by:
- Providing funding for the Global Security Contingency Fund
- Increasing funding for the State Partnership Program and the Asia-Pacific Regional Center

The Department continues its sustained growth in special operations forces to meet the expanding threat from terrorism and increase partnership building activities (Annex J).

SEEK A READY FORCE

The U.S. military has experienced four prior drawdowns in defense spending since the end of World War II, all of which resulted in disproportionate losses of capability. The force was maintained at a size and operated at a rate much higher than anticipated, and advisable, relative to overall funding levels. Consequently, resources had to come from other defense accounts leading to serious gaps in military readiness (Annex E). When circumstances changed and new conflicts emerged, large infusions of money were required to restore the health of the force.

In conceiving the new strategic concept, the DoD leadership was determined not to repeat the mistakes of the past, and have therefore structured this budget drawdown to protect readiness and avoid a "hollowing" of the military, a scenario in which the resources available for training, operations and maintenance are not adequate relative to the size of the force. The Department's new readiness model will accept risk by determining:

- How large a force can be maintained relative to resource levels
- How much of the force must be at peak-levels of readiness all of the time
- How quickly the remainder of the "less-ready" force can be brought up to war-fighting standard

Full-Spectrum Training Supported

Even with flat and declining defense budgets, the military is pressing ahead with its transition from a counterinsurgency-focused force to a force ready and capable of operating across a full range of operations. The service budgets all fund a return to full-spectrum training and preparation for missions beyond current operations in Afghanistan:

- The Army is preparing for a rotational presence in multiple regions and has begun training in "decisive action" scenarios and transitioning to training in combined arms warfare;
- The Marine Corps is returning to a sea-going posture, its traditional role in between major land wars;
- The Navy is investing in ship maintenance and measures to alleviate the stress on personnel from prolonged and extended deployments required by current operations;
- The Air Force is re-focusing on high-end capabilities required to confront advanced air forces and air defense systems of other nations.

The Department continues its work to understand and quantify readiness activities as we move into a post-conflict environment with increasing budgetary pressures. Specifically, the

Department is developing metrics by which we can better measure readiness levels to help identify critical readiness deficiencies. The planned improvements to readiness have been put at risk with the implementation of the FY 2013 sequester. The Department will continue to assess these impacts to better understand how sequestration will affect readiness in the future.

Under the existing budget program — not accounting for sequestration — sufficient funds will be available to maintain acceptable readiness for the planned size and mix of active and reserve forces. If, however, the Department continues to face sequester-level budget reductions at the magnitude currently prescribed in law, readiness will deteriorate.

PEOPLE ARE CENTRAL

A high-quality all-volunteer force continues to be the foundation of our military. But the cost of military personnel has grown at an unsustainable rate over the last decade. Including wartime funding, military personnel costs have nearly doubled since 2001, or about 35% above inflation, while the number of full-time military personnel, including activated reserves, increased by less than 2% during the same time period. In order to avoid disproportionate and dangerous additional cuts in force structure or modernization, the DoD continues to address the growth of personnel-related costs while keeping in mind that:

- Military life, irrespective of service, specialty, or deployment record always entails unique challenges and stresses.
- War-related deployments of the past decade have put extraordinary demands on many troops and their families, though the portion of the force that has been deployed to Iraq or Afghanistan declines every year.

To this end, the Department continued to support programs in FY 2014 that support service members and their families, including:

- *Transition Assistance and Veteran's Employment Assistance* — the Department continues to support the Transition Assistance Program (TAP) to ensure every service member receives training, education, and credentials needed to successfully transition to the civilian workforce. This includes a joint DoD-VA effort to redesign TAP.
- *Behavioral Health* — the Department maintains funding for psychological health programs and expands those programs that are most effective, such as Embedded Behavioral Health, to provide improved access to care, improved continuity of care, and enhanced behavioral health provider communication.
- *Family Readiness* — the Department continues to ensure that family support is a high priority by redesigning and boosting family support in a number of ways.

- *Suicide Prevention* — the Department continues to implement recommendations from the Suicide Prevention Task Force and act on other findings from various think tanks and, the National Action Alliance's National Suicide Prevention Strategy, and DoD and Department of Veteran's Affairs (VA) Integrated Mental Health Strategy (IMHS).
- *Sexual Assault* — the Department continues to implement a variety of initiatives to change the way it confronts sexual assault. These reforms are specifically intended to strengthen efforts in victim advocacy and accountability.

CONCLUSION

The choices made in the FY 2014 submission reflects the Department's intent to deepen the budget and program alignment with the President's strategic guidance, seek additional taxpayer savings where possible and prudent, and do so at minimum risk to the readiness or quality of the All-Volunteer Force.

As with the FY 2013 budget and the new strategic guidance that informed it, this request continues to seek to:
- Balance competing and compelling demands of supporting troops still engaged in Afghanistan;
- Protect readiness;
- Modernize the military's aging weapons inventory in keeping with the President's strategic guidance; and
- Sustain the quality and care of the All-Volunteer Force.

The Defense Department can, and must, continue to find new ways to operate more affordably and efficiently. However, multiple reviews and analyses show that additional major cuts — especially those on the scale and timeline of sequestration — would require dramatic reductions in core military capabilities. Indeed, reductions on this scale would require the Department to manage risk, readiness, and mission requirements in a fundamentally different way than the U.S. military has been accustomed to since the end of the Cold War. It would also require a re-thinking of America's security obligations and role in the world.

Our hope and expectation is that the department will receive some clarity and certainty about its immediate and mid-term budget future — certainty that will allow the U.S. military to set the priorities that will do right by those who serve, while protecting the most essential security interests of the American people.

ANNEXES

A. SPACE

In the FY 2014 budget, the Department needed to make improvements in its space portfolio. During the last half century, the United States has become increasingly reliant on our space capabilities for communications, navigation, and intelligence — yet our enemies are increasingly developing the ability to target our space capabilities.

Space provides global access, persistence, and capacity that cannot be obtained efficiently by air, sea, or ground based assets. As the barrier to entry has lowered, more actors are taking to space to reap these same benefits. The net result is a space environment that is becoming increasingly congested and contested.

These strategic shifts have prompted a series of enhancements to the U.S. military's space portfolio, investments further supported by the FY 2014 budget submission. In this budget we improve our capabilities to defend space, degrade enemy space capabilities, and operate through a degraded space environment.

Space Defense
- Additional sensors and analysts to provide the situational awareness and foundational intelligence that support space operations.
- Enhancing and expanding the Space Protection Program to provide better insight and analysis.
- Jam-resistant technologies and new operating concepts that will enhance the survivability of U.S satellites.

Degrade Enemy Space Capabilities
- Capabilities to deny or degrade potential adversaries' access to information.

Operate Through a Degraded Space Environment.
- Alternative capabilities in other domains to mitigate interruptions of U.S space assets.
- Enhancing training opportunities to ensure that our forces are better prepared to operate through space outages.

These investments were made possible by reallocating resources within the space portfolio, taking advantage of savings from acquisition reform.
- Better buying power initiatives and efficient contracting practices yielded over $400 million in FYDP savings from the communications portfolio that was used to fund space protection efforts.

- A new acquisition strategy for space launch yielded over $900 million in FYDP savings that went to achieve wholeness in space and other USAF space-related programs.
- The PB14 budget maintains investments in next-generation missile-warning, ISR, navigation, and communications capabilities.

B.   CYBER

Increases in the frequency and magnitude of cyberspace threats require further enhancement in DoD's cyber capabilities. The information and connectivity made available by the military's networks provides an asymmetric advantage to warfighters and are critical in the execution of all plans. The FY 2014 budget submission funds the re-organization of existing cyber forces into teams that will specialize in these three functions:

Defend Networks.   Cyber protection teams will be responsible for continually identifying and probing the weaknesses in network defenses, implementing fixes, and testing the results. The teams will be assigned to protect DoD Enterprise, Service and Combatant Commander networks.

Degrade Adversary Cyber Capabilities. Cyber combat mission teams will complement and enable Combatant Commanders' operational plans by supporting information campaigns, enabling our conventional forces, or negating an adversary's cyber forces.

Support Defense of National Infrastructure. National mission teams will be trained, equipped and postured to detect, deter, and, if called upon, respond to threats in cyberspace against critical infrastructure and to assist in securing federal and critical commercial systems. These forces will work hand-in-hand with the DHS.

The new teams will operate under USCYBERCOM concepts of employment, with each team dedicated to a specific mission.   Direct support teams will be established to provide additional analytic capacity and regional expertise for the national and combat mission teams. These new cyber teams will become operational starting in FY 2013.

We are creating these teams by re-organizing existing cyberspace personnel. Manpower from within the services and across DoD — military and civilian — will be re-assigned to grow the capacity of the cyber teams.   DoD will grow the cyberspace workforce by re-assigning non-cyber military billets to staff the new teams. This step reflects our need to accept risk in other military mission areas to close the cyber gap. More DoD civilians and contractors will also be assigned to provide support for the cyber effort. By FY 2016 the new cyber-force will consist of 40 mission teams, 25 direct support teams, and 68 protection teams.

Finally, we added resources to increase the quality and throughput of our training pipeline. Growing and retaining a skilled cyberforce is one of the biggest gaps in the cyberspace mission area. Accordingly, DoD has added resources to improve the quality of cyberspace training and support the increased volume of personnel that will need to be trained, especially over the next three to four years as the size of our cyber force increases. DoD also has committed to implementing a new cyberspace workforce management plan to ensure we can develop, retain, and promote our critical cyber workforce.

C. CIVILIAN PERSONNEL

The number of civilians in DoD will decline by about five percent over the FYDP. Defense budgets are constrained and additional savings are needed to increase some key modernization investments in keeping with the new defense strategy.

The Department of Defense relies on its civilian workforce to perform a variety of key missions in support of our military. From 2001 to 2013, civilian full-time equivalents grew by roughly 15 percent, from approximately 700,000 to a little more than 800,000. This includes United States and foreign national direct hires, as well as foreign national indirect hires. This growth occurred while the country was prosecuting two wars; new war-fighter domains such as cyber and unmanned intelligence, surveillance, and reconnaissance emerged; and the global security and geo-political risk environment changed significantly.

There is not a direct relationship between the drawdown of military end strength and the number of DoD civilians — they perform different functions. Civilian employment is much more a function of the number of military bases and the size of the depot workload rather than the number of military personnel.

The Department's five percent reduction in civilian personnel assumes future reductions in depot demands as the military withdraws from Afghanistan — after we reset the force — and a decrease in the number of DoD bases as part of a planned 2015 Base Realignment and Closure (BRAC). In addition, the services and agencies, especially the Defense Health Program, are achieving civilian personnel reductions through programmed restructuring initiatives.

Changes in the civilian workforce preserve mission-essential skills and abilities over the long term, while still shaping our civilian workforce in a way that is consistent with U.S defense strategy and continued fiscal pressures. This budget maintained civilians for key initiatives such as Navy carrier support, the Integrated Disability Evaluation System (IDES) assistance for service members, cyber security missions, and Special Operations Command.

D.   MILITARY PERSONNEL

Ground forces will continue to decrease this year and over the FYDP, with the size of the active Army dropping to 490,000 by FY 2017 and the active Marine Corps decreasing to 182,100 in FY 2017. The Air Force will execute a rebalancing of the size of its active, reserve and guard forces in accordance with the FY 2013 NDAA. The Navy is staying about the same size in total, making modest end strength reductions in its reserve forces and slightly growing the active component.

Trimming force structure that is excess to strategic requirements will free up funds to ensure a ready, modernized, and well-equipped military. The end strength cuts discussed here are driven by the defense strategy, which deemphasizes large, protracted, and manpower-intensive stability operations. However, the significant growth in the cost of military personnel — pay and benefits — may necessitate further cuts in force structure to help us achieve our defense strategy. In order to afford a ready and capable force in the future, DoD must slow the growth of military compensation.

The FY 2017 active troop levels represent a net reduction of 64,000 total Army end strength and 15,000 total Marine Corps end strength compared to FY 2012. These cuts, made in the FY 2013 President's Budget (PB13), reverse most of the growth in end strength that was needed to fight the wars in Afghanistan and Iraq and will save the Department billions of dollars per year. Even with these decreases, ground forces will be slightly larger than in 2001.

Making these manpower reductions — and achieving these savings — is necessary in order to transform ground forces stressed from over a decade of combat operations into an Army and Marine Corps postured for the national security challenges of the future.

The Department also made adjustments in Air Force end strength, which were subsequently modified in response to concerns of Congress and the Council of Governors. The rationale for the PB13 adjustments was based on eliminating excess go-to-war (surge) capacity, while ensuring DoD maintained sufficient forces to respond to continued high day-to-day demands. Total Air Force end strength drops by about 5,000 from FY 2013 to FY 2017.

The cost of military personnel has grown significantly over the last 10 years. From 2001 to 2012, military manpower costs doubled, from $97 billion to $195 billion, while end strength increased only moderately.

In order to afford our future force, DoD must contain the unsustainable costs of military personnel. The FY 2014 budget submission proposes:

- Slowing the projected growth in military pay with a proposed increase of 1% for FY 2014.
- Modest increases in TRICARE fees and co-payments for retirees and family members to reduce growth in the Department's $50 billion per year healthcare programs.

Finally, the Department is hopeful that the FY 2013 NDAA-directed Military Compensation and Retirement Modernization Commission can recommend feasible reforms to the costly military retirement program.

E.   READINESS

Our military faces many readiness challenges as it prepares for the future and withdraws from Afghanistan during a time of significant budget reductions. The U.S. military is exceptionally prepared for the counter-insurgency and counter-terrorism missions they have undertaken since 2001. They now must take steps to prepare for the full spectrum of challenges. The FY 2014 budget begins the process of restoring the force's ability to conduct the full range of military operations as required by the current defense strategy.

To be clear, we are not "re-setting" the force. Rather, we are preparing the force for a new and complex future of both national and trans-national threats. For example:

- Each of the Services must incorporate both wartime experience, such as how to operate in an increasingly joint, interagency and multinational environment, with new or expanded mission sets, such as medium-altitude intelligence, surveillance and reconnaissance.
- The Army is fundamentally changing the composition and management of its forces, by changing their force generation process, changing the composition of their Brigade Combat Teams, and beginning to regionally align some of its forces. These changes focus on building rapidly deployable contingency capabilities in support of the Combatant Commanders.
- The Navy, Air Force and Marine Corps expect there to be continued high demand for forward presence for some time following the withdrawal from Afghanistan, though the missions are more likely to involve training with partners, deterring instability and responding to crises rather than prolonged combat operations.

As the military make this transition over the next few years, the Department is keenly aware of the dangers of creating a "hollow force," the result of keeping more force structure than we can afford to keep ready. At the same time, we need a versatile and capable force that will require investments in readiness.

Historically, readiness has suffered during periods of downsizing, but the Department is committed to not only protecting readiness, but to creating a versatile and capable force. To do so, DoD must reshape the force structure, refocus training programs, reset and modernize equipment, reduce maintenance backlogs, and continue to recruit and retain high quality service members. In the FY 2014 budget:

- The Air Force rebalanced the allocation of flying hours across their force to maintain, and in some cases, improve readiness levels. They also increased funding for training ranges and weapon system sustainment.

- The Navy added manpower necessary to support new platforms, including AEGIS Ashore, the Littoral Combat Ship and the increasing number of unmanned platforms operated at sea. The Navy also increased the number of sailors assigned to Regional Maintenance Centers, supporting both current maintenance requirements and paying future readiness dividends when these experienced maintainers return to sea.
- The Marine Corps increased funds for unit readiness, primarily for Asia-Pacific rebalance and full-spectrum training.

The Department is actively managing how to generate the ready forces needed to support the defense strategic guidance. The DoD is determining how much of the force must be fully ready all of the time and how quickly the remainder of the force can be made ready. For example, the defense strategy does not require all forces to be ready all the time — some have to deploy immediately, while others are not needed until 90, 120, or even 180 days into a conflict. Some capabilities take longer to generate than others — for these reasons, force generation processes naturally vary across force elements.

To examine these issues, the Department has constituted a Readiness Management Group to investigate how the strategy (which tells us "what to be ready for") translates into the readiness levels needed to execute it ("how ready we need to be"), and then work with the services to design processes to generate those levels of readiness.

The current sequestered budget levels are impacting operational readiness in significant ways. Further work must be done to understand the longer term impacts of these short term cuts to operations and maintenance funds. The FY 2014 President's Budget was not developed to account for the FY 2013 shortfall, and the Department must do more to understand these impacts.

F.   MUNITIONS

The Department of Defense, Congress, and the media tend to focus on platforms — the number of carriers, the type of aircraft, or the capability of a ground vehicle.   However, regardless of the number of platforms or the advancement of technological capabilities on our platforms, we cannot credibly deter nor can we effectively defeat adversaries without munitions.

Even though munitions are critically important, in order to meet the budget, we too often have considered munitions as an afterthought or, more worrisome, as a bill payer. This is a mistake. Weapon delivery platforms are of no value without munitions, so this budget deliberately protects and even enhances development and procurement of munitions, increasing both capability and capacity.

Our military's weapons must be invulnerable to countermeasures and be able to out-reach our enemy's defenses. Potential adversaries continue to improve their capabilities, challenging our ability to project power, especially in anti-access environments. In order to preserve tactical, operational, and strategic advantages, the FY 2014 submission increased investments in munitions that overcome and resist adversary countermeasures, outrange enemy weapons, and strike difficult targets. For example, this budget:

- Increased procurement of advanced blocks of air-to-air missiles like AIM-9X
- Funded development and production of a new highly capable, long-range anti-ship cruise missile designed to out-range and resist adversary countermeasures
- Increased procurement of extended range Joint Air-to-Surface Standoff Missiles (JASSM-ER) to enhance our arsenal of advanced long-range strike missiles
- Funded improvements to weapons designed to destroy or defeat hard and deeply buried targets, such as the BLU-109 and BLU-113 penetrators
- Funded development of a new increment of the Guided Multiple Launch Rocket System (GMLRS) designed to strike targets at range from the ground
- Funded a service life extension for the existing Army Tactical Missile System (ATACMS) to bridge the gap until the new GMLRS increment is fielded and comply with our cluster munitions policy

We also enhanced capability and effective capacity by integrating munitions on a broader set of platforms, funding demonstrations to expand applications of existing munitions, and ensuring that the right munitions were strategically located around the world. For example, we:
- Integrated long-range air-launched JASSM-ERs on additional aircraft

- Integrated advanced Small Diameter Bombs (SDB-II) with all-weather and moving target capability on additional Navy aircraft
- Funded development and demonstrations of alternative uses of existing capabilities, expanding delivery platform options as well as broadening the type of targets munitions are able to strike
- Adjusted the apportionment of munitions around the globe to align with the strategy, emphasizing our shift to the Asia-Pacific region

The Department is also expanding flexibility by continuing to export weapons to allies through foreign military sales, providing a critical opportunity to partner with our allies and increase interoperability by exporting munitions such as:

- AIM-120 and AIM-9 air-to-air weapons
- Joint Direct Attack Munition (JDAM) and Joint Stand-off Weapon (JSOW) air-to-ground weapons
- ATACMS and GMLRS ground-strike weapons
- Evolved NATO Sea Sparrow Missile (ESSM) and Harpoon maritime weapons

Investing in munitions is not enough. In order to support the strategy under a constrained budget, we need a healthy, flexible, and responsive industrial base. The time required to ramp up production continues to be lengthy. DoD is partnering with industry to investigate options to decrease the time required to ramp up production when needed and to increase efficiency.

The Department is also pursuing creative partnerships with industry and allies to increase development and production efficiency. The Harpoon anti-ship weapon is a great example of this type of creative partnership. While we have a sufficient number of existing Harpoons, advancing threats require a more capable missile. Instead of simply buying upgraded Harpoons, we are partnering with industry through a Sales Exchange Agreement to divest a limited number of legacy weapons in exchange for Harpoon II+ missile upgrade kits. Legacy missile components support ongoing sales of Harpoon missiles to allied and friendly nations while we receive Harpoon II+ missile kits at no additional cost. This initiative stabilizes the Harpoon industrial base, while upgrading missile performance, supporting our allies, and increasing US/International interoperability.

G.   ACTIVE COMPONENT/RESERVE COMPONENT (AC/RC)

In a pressured budgetary environment, it is critical that DoD maintain only the number of forces necessary to execute the strategy, and those forces must be assigned to the most appropriate component—active or reserve. DoD's actions have included the transfer, relocation, re-missioning, and when appropriate, retirement of various Active and Reserve Component capabilities. These actions have been informed by the need to ensure:

- Sufficient force posture to conduct Federal and State missions — including defense support to civil authorities
- The Total Force retains the ability to meet the warfighting requirements in the defense strategic guidance
- The Active and Reserve mix supports overseas day-to-day rotational requirements at sustainable rates
- The Active force retains the recruiting, training, and operational base to sustain a viable Total Force into the future
- The Reserve Components remain relevant and engaged in both enduring and evolving missions.

Last year, DoD made adjustments to the Active and Reserve Component structure to align the Total Force with the new strategy and to meet reduced fiscal topline:

- Active Army end strength will decline by 60,000 and National Guard end strength by 8,000, while authorizations in the Army Reserve will decrease by 1,000 to 205,000 between FY 2012 and FY 2017.
- Marine Corps Active end strength will decrease by 15,000 from FY 2012 and FY 2016. There is no change to the Marine Corps Reserves.
- Navy Active end strength increased by 3,400 between FY 2013 and FY 2018 to meet at-sea manning and cyber warfare requirements. Navy Reserve end strength declined by approximately 2,500 over the next five years due to decreased demand for expeditionary combat assets, specifically construction units in Afghanistan.

As the Department seeks the proper balance between Active and Reserve components, we must also account for the needs of states given the national guard's mission to provide defense support to civil authorities. Based on concerns from Congress and the Council of Governors, the Department modified its PB13 reductions to Air Force Active and Reserve Component aircraft and personnel.

- The original FY 2013 PB submission proposed reducing the Total Air Force aircraft inventory by 286 aircraft with 195 Air National Guard and Reserve Component aircraft reductions. These numbers were revised as a result of the FY 2013 NDAA and DoD's

PB14 budget submission to restore 117 aircraft to the Guard and Reserve through the end of FY 2014 and 74 aircraft beyond FY 2014.

- Of the approximately 7,000 Guard and Reserve military billets cut in the FY 2013 President's Budget, 4,200 Air National Guard billets were restored via the FY 2013 NDAA and appropriation and sustained in the FY 2014 PB submission.
- Accordingly, the total reduction of ANG and AF Reserve military billets from FY 2013 to FY 2017 is 1,300 for the ANG and 1,900 for the AF Reserve, for a total RC military end strength reduction of 3,200.
- Active end strength was reduced by 2000 between FY 2013 and FY 2018.

The Department is taking full advantage of the Chief of the National Guard Bureau, now a member of the Joint Chiefs, to define the requirements for the mix of missions performed by the National Guard. DoD is also working closely with the Council of Governors to better understand the link between their missions and requirements, by FEMA region, for Defense Support to Civil Authorities.

To address the Governors' future concerns about the impact of DoD budget decisions on the Reserve Components and State missions, the Department and the States are developing a sustained consultative process to exchange information and advice on civil support requirements. This process will help inform consideration of National Guard force structure and budget issues.

H.   NAVAL PRESENCE

The Department's new strategy calls for the U.S. military to be engaged globally to build partnerships and deter adversaries. It will be increasingly difficult to respond to a crisis if forces are not already in the vicinity. This puts a premium on presence.

The Navy provides global stabilizing presence by deploying naval forces to build relations with partner nations, demonstrate commitment to allies, deter potentially aggressive adversaries, counter terrorism, conduct humanitarian and disaster relief operations, and immediately project power in the event of war.

The Department identified ways to strategically invest in maintenance, personnel incentives, and forward basing to increase the amount of presence from existing forces. In particular, Carrier Strike Groups (CSGs), nuclear submarines, and Ballistic Missile Defense (BMD) capable surface ships.

Over the past three years the Navy has been asked to increase the deployment of CSGs to ensure U.S. capability for quick response to potential crises, averaging about three CSGs deployed at any time. This has stressed the force, resulting in a maintenance backlog affecting both aircraft carrier and submarine forces. To increase the level of readiness, DoD provided resources to critical nuclear shipyards, increasing manning by 10%.

This sustained high level of operations for CSGs (highest since the Vietnam War) also increases the stress on the crews and their families, risking reduced retention. To counter this, DoD:
- Increased special pays, such as Selective Reenlistment Bonuses (SRBs), to ensure we are able to retain a proper balance of qualified middle and senior level officers and enlisted.
- Provided funds to increase accessions of personnel into the nuclear training pipeline, ensuring that our nuclear-trained sailors can properly crew our vessels in the future.

These investments represent only a first step in addressing CSG presence issues. More analysis and potentially more funding will be required over the next few years if CSG deployments remain at these elevated levels.

DoD invested in Pacific bases in Guam and Pearl Harbor to enhance our capacity for submarine and CSG operations and to support our rebalancing to the Asia-Pacific region:
- The Department added $78 million in FY 2014 to enable basing of another fast-attack submarine in Guam.

- The Department also added $300 million across the FYDP to dredge Pearl Harbor to ease aircraft carrier access.

The Department will procure a second Virginia-Class attack submarine in FY 2014; this will lessen the impact from the retirements of Los Angeles-Class attack submarines in the 2020s.

In PB13, the Department started its plan to increase BMD support to Europe (as part of the Phased Adaptive Approach) by homeporting four BMD ships in ROTA Spain. Two will report there in FY 2014, followed by two more in FY 2015. With a shorter distance to station and the enhanced/shorter maintenance cycle used by overseas-homeported ships, they will markedly increase the BMD presence in Europe.

I. STRATEGIC DEFENSE AND DETERRENT

The Department will maintain a strong nuclear deterrence posture in the face of all potential threats, including developments in North Korea and risks from Iran. We are also committed to providing effective missile defense and maintaining a safe, secure, and effective nuclear arsenal. Despite budget pressures, DoD has ensured robust funding for these mission areas, making investments and taking actions to ensure the U.S. remains ahead of threat developments, including:

- Refocusing technologically advanced systems unlikely to be fielded quickly towards tech development activities to reduce risk and cost but that will field later (SM-3 IIB)
- Cancelling expensive surveillance systems and reinvesting in achievable, near-term upgrades to ground based radars (PTSS)
- Adding to national hedge against ballistic missile attack from rogue states (GBIs)
- Partnering with the National Nuclear Security Agency (NNSA) to assess the true requirements of the nuclear stockpile and associated infrastructure.

SM-3 IIB. The SM-3 IIB missile defense interceptor was previously planned to be based in Europe and provide an additional capability to defend the U.S. from ballistic missile attack. Given the advancing threat posed by North Korea in particular, the DoD assessed that the SM-3 IIB would be late to need and therefore restructured the program by reinvesting the funds into advanced interceptor technology development to include a common kill vehicle, and other enabling programs. The restructuring also funds the increased number of Ground Based Interceptors (GBIs), from 30 to 44. The SM-3 IIB program would have provided an expensive niche capability while homeland defense gaps widen. Changing the investment strategy to advanced technology development and additional deployment of GBIs will better address current and future threat challenges.

Precision Tracking Space Sensor. PTSS was intended to be a constellation of satellites to track medium and intermediate range ballistic missiles as well as intercontinental ballistic missiles. A review of the program found significant cost growth, schedule concurrency, technical risk, and utility concerns. Therefore, DoD terminated the PTSS program and reinvested some of the savings in evolutionary upgrades to existing systems. Reinvesting PTSS funds addresses key sensor gaps, including discrimination, raid size, and coverage. These investments provide upgrades to existing radars and strengthen operational support of missile defense systems.

Ground Based Interceptors. GBIs are missile interceptors based in Alaska and California, intended to defend the U.S. from limited ballistic missile attack. Restructure of the SM-3 IIB program allowed for additional buys of 14 GBIs and corresponding refurbishment of the

Alaskan missile field at Fort Greely. This restructure decision was driven by increased concerns and intelligence regarding the current threat environment. The increase in GBIs closes the near-term gap between our defense capabilities and threat intelligence projections.

Partnering with the Department of Energy. In addition to missile defense, DoD partnered with the Department of Energy's National Nuclear Security Agency to assess nuclear stockpile and infrastructure requirements. As an outcome, the DoD and DoE better postured the nation to ensure an executable, safe nuclear weapons program for years to come by:

- Funding maintenance, upgrades, and replacements for aging nuclear infrastructure.
- Finding cost-effective approaches to extending the life of our nuclear arsenal without compromising safety, security, or effectiveness.
- Robustly funding a broad array of non-proliferation projects to reduce global nuclear dangers.
- Restructuring efforts for disposition of excess plutonium on a path to ensure efforts are both effective and fiscally responsible.
- Initiating efforts to gain numerous efficiencies across the enterprise.

J.   SPECIAL OPERATIONS FORCES (SOF)

The Department protected its long-planned growth of Special Operations Forces (SOF) in the FY 2014 budget submission, with the growth across the Department's FYDP mainly enhancing SOF enablers.

Global counterterrorism efforts since 9/11 have significantly increased the demand for SOF. Thousands of SOF personnel are deployed around the world at any given time strengthening relationships, building partner capacity, and countering insurgencies, violent extremism, weapons of mass destruction, and transnational criminal networks.

Growing SOF end strength from fewer than 40,000 in 2001 to more than 66,000 today, has helped mitigated the stress from the high tempo of operations and demand for SOF forces.

A lesson learned after 9/11 is that the Department cannot "surge" SOF personnel to meet contingencies. Consequently, PB14 protects the planned growth of SOF forces, including enablers such as intelligence, aviation, and civil affairs personnel, in addition to operators. PB14 puts emphasis on ensuring that SOF personnel will remain highly ready. Ongoing efforts to replace and update SOF equipment are continued, ensuring that forces have the appropriate systems needed to operate in remote and austere conditions. In particular, we have made improvements throughout the SOF aircraft portfolio, increasing the capabilities of gunships, helicopters, and intelligence aircraft.

As the counterterrorism threat continues to expand globally, SOF personnel will be confronted with pent up demand — in Africa and Southeast Asia especially — that has not been met due to commitments in Afghanistan. SOF will play a crucial and expanding role in developing the capabilities of our international partners to thwart the spread of global terrorism and prevent hostilities from turning into major regional conflicts.

It is uncertain what new threats the U.S. may face in the coming years. However, it is clear that the small-footprint, innovative approaches that our SOF operators have developed in the past decade will play a significant role in combating current and future threats. We will be prepared to face these unknowns with a SOF force that is sized, trained, and equipped to achieve our nation's security objectives.

K.   INTELLIGENCE, SURVEILLANCE, AND RECONNAISSANCE (ISR)

The FY 2014 Program Review re-examined current and future Intelligence, Surveillance, and Reconnaissance (ISR) needs to ensure ISR investments are sufficient and appropriately balanced. This entailed preserving the capabilities needed to conduct current core missions while making investments to support both emerging challenges in the Middle East and a rebalance toward the Asia-Pacific.

The MQ-1 Predators and MQ-9 Reapers have been, and will continue to be, our counter-insurgency and counter-terrorism workhorses. DoD continues building toward a fleet of 65 Reaper orbits to support counter-terrorism and other missions described in the new strategy. Predators and Reapers, however, have range and survivability limitations, and therefore depend on access to nearby bases and cannot operate in locations protected by modern air defenses.

As the U.S. military draws down in Afghanistan, longer range capabilities will be needed to support operations from more distant bases. Consequently, the FY 2014 budget submission invests in extending the range of the Reaper with a longer wing and external fuel tank to substantially increase range.

Land-based ISR platforms can be modified to extend range, but may still be limited by host-nation demands at the more distant bases. To further lessen dependence on forward basing, we invested in a near-term, relatively low-cost, sea-base Reaper-like capability, called the Unmanned Carrier-Launched Surveillance and Strike (UCLASS) program. Cost and capability trades are currently under investigation in an update to the UCLASS Analysis of Alternatives.

Finally, DoD protected and, in some cases, enhanced investments in future Anti-Access, Area Denial (A2AD) ISR to mitigate the limitations imposed by modern air defenses on current capabilities. The Department is re-prioritizing the Science and Technology portfolio to focus on evolutionary capabilities that can be delivered relatively soon rather than revolutionary, advancements that may take decades to realize.

L.   ENERGY

DoD is the single largest consumer of energy in the U.S., spending about $22 billion per year on energy. Additionally, energy needs continue to constrain the U.S. military's operational capabilities. Large energy consumption creates long logistic tails that are vulnerable to attack. This energy demand constrains the capabilities of our ground, air, and sea forces at home and abroad. For example, refueling needs limit the abilities of our soldiers, range of our aircraft, and the time-on-station of our ships.

The Department must find ways to reduce energy costs and become more efficient. In the FY 2014 budget submission, DoD continues to invest in metering and alternative energy sources like solar. There is a new focus on energy efficiency in for the Department's infrastructure rehabilitation projects. This budget includes investments in research and development for more efficient ship and aircraft engines, longer-lived batteries for our ground-based communications systems, lighter batteries for troops to carry, and alternative energy sources to lessen dependence on oil in the future. These investments are grouped into three major categories.

Primary investments make immediate sense from an economic and operational standpoint. For example, to reduce facility energy costs we are investing in metering, insulating buildings, and installing high efficiency heating and cooling systems. Over the next seven years these improvements are expected to result in $1.5 billion savings annually by 2020. They also support compliance mandates associated with maintaining DoD's approximately 300,000 buildings. This budget funds and builds Renewable Energy projects (wind, solar, and hydro) to improve energy security in a cost effective manner.

Ancillary investments are not driven primarily by energy-efficiency concerns, but they do benefit the Department by reducing fuel costs. For example, transmissions in Bradley fighting vehicles are being replaced with newer models that provide three percent improved fuel efficiency. Much of the HMMWV (Humvee) fleet is being replaced with the more fuel-efficient Joint Light Tactical Vehicle (JLTV).

Developmental investments are made to garner a significant return on investment or enhance the military's technological edge. DoD is making a concerted effort to incorporate energy plans into the design of every single future development effort, such as more efficient engines for aircraft and ships, longer-life batteries, and alternative energy sources.

M.   INDUSTRIAL BASE & THE OFFICE OF ECONOMIC ADJUSTMENT

The Department modified, reduced, delayed, or cancelled many acquisition programs in the FY 2014 budget submission in order to meet the defense spending cuts established in the Budget Control Act of 2011. These changes will affect the defense industrial base and, in some cases, adversely affect the communities directly surrounding key research and development or manufacturing facilities.

The Department is constantly observing the effects of program budget decisions on its suppliers. The FY 2014 budget request provides funding for projects to sustain critical niche industrial base capabilities not found or realistically replaced in the civilian sector. In some cases the need for these critical capabilities may span multiple acquisition programs, or fall outside of the responsibility of any one specific program. The funding will be used to support the highest priority technologies and skills that are most vulnerable to production breaks and funding reductions, particularly at the sub-tier supplier level. These funds will be administered to ensure that any breaks in production are reversible.

The FY 2014 budget request also increases funding to assist communities affected by procurement cuts. Through its Office of Economic Adjustment, the Department will help communities organize, plan, and carry-out local adjustment and diversification strategies through grants and technical assistance. The Department will also assist in coordinating a federal response to help communities secure federal resources for workforce training, entrepreneurial training, small business counseling, and business planning services.

www.ingramcontent.com/pod-product-compliance
Lightning Source LLC
Chambersburg PA
CBHW080744290526
45790CB00008B/3313